THE T-RRIBLE

BY J.N. PAQUET

Somewhere over some magnificent land and seascapes,
A flying object flew past some cliffs and hill shapes.
As yellow as a yolk, as white as a milk glass,
Landed in a swishy sound as it touched the grass.

A tiny two-mouth monster jumped off the spaceship,
His long space travel made him wobbly on his feet.
His name was *The T-RRIBLE*. What a name that is!
No scary monster, rather a colourful squeeze.

His space travel had been very tiring,
Our little monster needed exercising.
*"Arms up and arms down... To the left and to the right...
Jump up and jump up... Grab your toes and hold tight!"*

Walking on the wetly muddy soft grass felt strange,
For every step he made, there was a sound change.
Smushy-smush! Smooshy-smush! Smishy-smush! Smashy-smush!
But *The T-RRIBLE* really was in a rush.

Long walk in the country, then he found the city,
Discovering our world, different, yet pretty.
In a street, he stopped by a strange grey creature,
With three colour changing eyes. What a funny picture!

He asked an old lady *"What is that thing, please?"*
She answered smiling: *"The traffic lights, my cream cheese!"*
But a single glance at him caused her quite a stir,
She started running away, screaming *"Monster! Monster!"*

"Why, she seemed quite afraid of that creature!
I should hurry before it starts moving, for sure!"
Looking both ways, he crossed the street very carefully,
No running, no screaming, just a mindful worry.

A quick walk later, he stopped in a narrow street,
A little house. At a window, some marguerites.
"Number 5, Canada Street. It's here, I know it!"
He knocked at the door, impatient to meet and greet.

As the door opened rapidly, a wind blew out,
A smiling little boy and his mummy stepped out.
The boy was Oliver Bluemoon. One of the kindest,
"I've got some T-RRIBLE news! Things couldn't be worse..."

"A huge asteroid will destroy my planet!"
The little monster waved pictures on his tablet.
"Only YOU can save us from the danger ahead!"
The T-RRIBLE very seriously said.

"Why me?" Oliver asked. *"How can I save your planet?"*
"I'm too small. There must be someone else you forget!"
But *The T-RRIBLE* answered with a big smile,
"To us, you are really special, someone worthwhile!"

*"See, on my planet and in the entire galaxy,
Some speak a language that is easy to me.
And some use other words and other phrases,
But no one has ever spoken two languages!"*

"YOU speak two languages! That's what makes you so special!
Please, come with me on a very quick travel.
Tell our leaders we need to help each other,
If we act together, we'll prevent the danger!"

After the little monster's convincing talk,
Oliver knew he had to be brave and walk.
From the smallest boy in London we can see,
The hero of this story he was meant to be.

His Mummy, worried, stared at the monster for a while,
Could she let her boy go to that planet, with a smile?
The T-RRIBLE was just about Oliver's height,
Terrible was his name, but he was nice and polite.

Well, she did give him the thumbs up in the end,
After all, her little boy had to help his new friend.
Oliver and the monster headed to the garden,
Where they stood in a puddle, their boots on, and then...

The T-RRIBLE placed a stone on Oliver's left hand,
Asking him to close his eyes, he would soon understand.
*"Think about the stars and let the stone fall,
A door will appear before us, then a large entrance hall."*

"It is a shortcut, a passage to my planet,
We can only use it once, it is a secret!"
Stepping through the door, floating in a peculiar way,
They landed on *T-RRIBLE 4*, the very same day.

The green planet was no different from Oliver's,
A couple of clouds, some endless fields and two rivers.
However, there were honey trees everywhere,
And some little monsters running in despair.

"Look, Oliver! Look how scared they all are!
We must hurry and act against that falling star!"
The two little friends ran through the green cotton grass,
To meet with *King ADO-RABLE* in his Great Palace.

No guards at the gates as they too had ran away,
They found the King crying, on his own, in a walkway.
Much to his dismay, everyone had left the place,
He alone had decided to stay, just in case.

*"Your Majesty, my friend Oliver will help you,
He speaks our language and the other one too!"*
The King had never heard of such a thing,
To be able to speak two languages, that was amazing!

"How can we stop the asteroid?" Oliver asked,
The King showed him a mountain that a dark cloud masked.
*"The Dark King, from the other land, must use his laser,
Together with ours, only that could end the danger."*

Whilst on their way to the dark side of the planet,
Oliver taught them some words they would never forget.
The T-RRIBLE and the King were both happy to learn,
Those words in a language they could at last discern.

" 'Bonjour' means 'Hello' and 'Merci' means 'Thank you.' "
Oliver told his companions who were smiling too.
Climbing that mountain was not effortless,
But the real effort was to learn and progress.

When they reached the Dark Palace of *King HO-RRIBLE*,
The same scenes of chaos were repeated overall.
There too they found the Dark King all alone,
Staring at a bright light in the sky, seated on his throne.

« *Qui êtes-vous?* » The Dark King blasted,
"Who are you?" Oliver said he had asked.
Then, started the first ever chat between the two Kings,
Who actually were brothers of fifty-five springs.

Oliver was there, explaining to the two Kings,
How it was just fair, how easy were these things.
That team work was essential to save their planet,
They were both equal, like two singers in a duet.

*"Target the asteroid with your laser pointer,
The strength of the two beams will divert it together."*
The Dark King accepted to try the trick,
He had nothing to lose or else cause a panic.

Then, they agreed on a specific timing,
Each one in their homeland, the laser pointing.
The clock struck nine when the emissions started,
They hit the rock and diverted it, as expected.

"We did it!" *The T-RRIBLE* screamed, jumping up and down,
"It worked so well, we have even melted it down!"
The Kings thanked Oliver for his assistance,
The green planet owed him its precious existence.

A party was given in the little boy's honour,
On *T-RRIBLE 4*, honey was flowing like water.
Everyone was celebrating the happy ending,
Oliver, *the T-RRIBLE* and even the two Kings.

The Kings promised they would all learn how to spell,
When finally time came to say farewell.
With a chalk, *The T-RRIBLE* drew a door on a wall,
Another passage, to Earth this time, once and for all.

"Farewell my friend!" The T-RRIBLE said, all smiles,
"Not forever, we will meet again once in a while."
When the little boy stepped through the magical door,
He found himself back home, a few minutes before.

It looked as if nothing had ever happened,
For it was in his room that he had at last returned.
He ran down the stairs when the bell rang again at the door,
Alas, no monster. But a medal with an engraved... number four.

THE END

FROM THE SAME AUTHOR:

OVER 50 BOOKS IN MONO, BILINGUAL & TRILINGUAL FORMATS
AVAILABLE AT: WWW.JNPAQUET-BOOKS.COM

THE BOOK OF THE ANIMALS (7 Books)
THE BOOK OF THE ANIMALS – mini (x7)
THE BOOK OF THE ANIMALS – COLLECTION (x3)
THE BOOK OF THE ANIMALS – SPECIALS (x3)
THE BOOK OF THE ANIMALS – SPIN-OFF (x4)
THE BOOK OF THE ANIMALS – COLOURING TOGETHER (x2)

HAPPY LITTLE LUKA (x2)

I JUST LOVE MONSTERS!
I JUST LOVE MY FRIENDS!
I JUST LOVE DINOSAURS!

MELY & BELA IN THE KINGDOM
OF THE BLUE STRAWBERRIES

WHEN EVERYTHING IS... LITTLE AND BLUE

MY FIRST SMARTBOOK

LITTLE CHARLIE VISITS LONDON

WAKEY WAKEY!

THE T-RRIBLE (x2)
THE mini T-RRIBLE (x2)

PRINCE GEORGE: NO BATH ON A MONDAY!

ONCE UPON A TOUR

JACOB & DAD – HUG IT OUT!

BABIES' DREAMS

This book is dedicated to Isabela, Amélie & Alex.

Copyright © 2013-2015 J.N. PAQUET. Characters, text & illustrations copyright.

The right of J.N. PAQUET to be identified as the Author of the Work has been asserted by him in accordance with the Copyright, Designs and Patent Act 1988. All rights reserved. No part of this publication may be reproduced, stored in a retrieval system, or transmitted, in any form or by any means without the prior written permission of the author, nor be otherwise circulated in any form of binding or cover other than that in which it is published and without a similar condition being imposed on the subsequent purchaser. To publish, republish, copy or distribute this book, please contact: contact@jnpaquet-books.com

"The T-RRIBLE" and JNPAQUET Books Ltd Publishing Rights © J.N. PAQUET.

"The T-RRIBLE" characters, names and related indicia are © 2013-2015, J.N. PAQUET - All rights reserved.

Copyright © 2015, JNPAQUET Books Ltd. All rights reserved. Special Edition.

J.N. PAQUET™ is a trade mark registered in the UK Register of Trade Marks, in the United Kingdom, under No. 2540865

ISBN 9781910909287 (PAPERBACK)
eISBN 9781910909294 (EBOOK)

www.ingramcontent.com/pod-product-compliance
Lightning Source LLC
Chambersburg PA
CBHW081129080526
44587CB00021B/3808